GLEN BAXTER

RETURNS TO
NORMAL

First published in 1992
Copyright © 1992 by Glen Baxter
The moral right of the author
has been asserted

Bloomsbury Publishing Ltd, 2 Soho Square, London W1V 5DE

A CIP catalogue record for this book
is available from the British Library

ISBN 0-7475-1349 X

Of the drawings in this collection, fifteen appeared originally
in *The New Yorker* and were copyrighted in the years 1989, 1990
and 1991 by *The New Yorker Magazine, Inc.*

Printed in Great Britain by Butler and Tanner Ltd, Frome

CONTENTS

To Ron Padgett & Tommy Duncan

ANTONY'S PROGRESS ON THE
CLARINET WAS PAINFULLY SLOW

I KNEW IT WAS AN OUTSIDE
CHANCE, BUT IF I COULD KEEP
THE ANTS IN LINE, WE MIGHT
JUST REACH CAMP MORESBY
BEFORE DAWN...

THERE WAS NOTHING ERIC LIKED
BETTER THAN AN EVENING ALONE
AT HOME WITH HIS TWINE

ROBINSON'S PLAN TO REACH THE
FINAL UNOPPOSED WAS SIMPLE,
YET REMARKABLY EFFECTIVE

THE TENSION AT Nº 83 HAD BEEN
ALMOST UNBEARABLE EVER
SINCE ERIC HAD DELIBERATELY
SWALLOWED TOBY'S ANORAK

"I'D LIKE YOU TO MEET THE FUTURE
MRS. BOSWORTH" ANNOUNCED SNOAD

THE TWINS WERE NOT NOTED FOR
THEIR LOVE OF FRESH VEGETABLES

I NEVER FULLY RECOVERED FROM THE
APPALLING SHOCK OF DISCOVERING MY
FATHER'S COLLECTION OF FLEETWOOD
MAC ALBUMS...

"WE'RE IN LUCK. THE ENTRANCE
TO THE SAFETY DEPOSIT VAULTS
IS ONLY PATROLLED EVERY
HALF HOUR!" GROWLED CELIA

"I THOUGHT WE HAD AGREED NOT TO DISCUSS
YOUR HUSBAND" SNAPPED CELIA

ALTHOUGH THERE SEEMED TO BE
A GENERAL LACK OF AMENITIES
I WAS FORTUNATE ENOUGH TO HAVE
BEEN MY GIVEN MY OWN BED...

ASKING SIMON TO LEND A HAND
IN THE KITCHEN WAS ALWAYS
A BIG MISTAKE...

"SO YOU FOUND THE BUTTER,
THEN?" GRUNTED KLAUS

I WOULD HAVE CHOSEN CARPET FOR
THE HALL, BUT BRENDA CLEARLY
HAD IDEAS OF HER OWN

WE CELEBRATED FATHER'S BIRTHDAY
IN THE TRADITIONAL MANNER

THE EVENING ENDED
ON A SOUR NOTE

"I'M AFRAID THIS HERALDS THE DAWN
OF A MAJOR NEW OFFENSIVE, MY LIEGE!"
ROARED THE RECEPTIONIST.

A GLANCE INTO THE KITCHEN CONFIRMED
MY DEEPEST SUSPICIONS. THEY WERE
COOKING THE OMELETTES "FLEMISH STYLE."

AFTER A FIERCE STRUGGLE, ROBIN
EVENTUALLY AGREED TO RELINQUISH
POSSESSION OF THE REMOTE CONTROL.

DURING A MOMENTARY LAPSE IN
CONCENTRATION, I EFFECTED MY
ESCAPE FROM MY CAPTORS...

"CAN I TAKE IT THAT THE ELECTRIC LUTE
IS NOT TO YOUR LIKING, MY LIEGE?" QUOTH ROBIN

WHEN IT CAME TO ENTERTAINMENT,
THERE WAS LITTLE TO MATCH
ERIC AND HIS DANCING CUCUMBER

"FEAR NOT, ROBIN YOU'RE SAFE IN MY HANDS!" CONFIDED THE OPTICIAN

ALONE IN HIS MOMENT OF
RAPTURE, RALPH RETURNED
ONCE AGAIN TO CONTEMPLATION
OF THE GOURD

HUBERT GAZED ON IN AWE AT
THE MORSEL

SIR HENRY OF HAWKSWOOD
TENDED TO PREFER A WALL-
MOUNTED SWIVEL ARM FITTING
WITH A PASTEL PLEATED SHADE

EVER SINCE THE ACCIDENTAL SINGEING
OF HIS DUFFLE COAT, ERIC HAD BECOME
MOROSE AND DECIDEDLY PETULANT

WHEN IT CAME TO OUTSIDE CATERING
THERE WAS NOTHING TO MATCH THE
UNERRING PRECISION OF ROBIN'S BLADE

IT LOOKED SUSPICIOUSLY LIKE THE
WORK OF YET ANOTHER LITTLE KNOWN
NINETEENTH CENTURY WATERCOLOURIST

HANK'S TOUR OF THE LOUVRE
USUALLY LASTED ALMOST
EIGHTEEN MINUTES.

ZEKE NEVER DID TAKE TOO
KINDLY TO DAHLIAS.

LUCKILY, THE INDUSTRIAL-STRENGTH
EARPLUGS I HAD PURCHASED IN
TUCSON WERE HOLDING UP WELL
AGAINST THE ONSLAUGHT.

HANK APPEARED TO BE HAVING A
LITTLE TROUBLE WITH THE
CONCEPT OF 'EGGS OVER EASY'.

THE BOYS ALWAYS FOUND SUNSET ON
THE PRAIRIE TO BE A PARTICULARLY
MOVING EXPERIENCE.

JED HAD ORGANIZED ANOTHER
OF HIS MINI-PROTESTS.

A WIND OF CHANGE WAS SWEEPING THROUGH
THE OLD BUNKHOUSE, AND ZEKE DIDN'T
CARE FOR IT ONE LITTLE BIT.

THE BARTENDER WAS A MOODY,
UNPREDICTABLE BELGIAN, WHOSE
KNOWLEDGE OF MARQUETRY WAS
RARELY, IF EVER, CALLED INTO QUESTION

"I KNOW IT'S A BAD DRAWING,
BUT THIS IS SUPPOSED TO BE
A STAR" GRUMBLED NED DRYLY

"BUT I CAN SURE BROIL A
DING-DANGED SWELL STEAK"
RETORTED DORIS

"I'M AFRAID WHAT THIS MEANS, YOUNG JIMMY
IS THAT TECHNICALLY YOU'RE A GONER..."

THERE WAS ALWAYS AN UNSEEMLY
RUSH FOR SEATS AT THE
CROCHET SEMINAR

TEX SPENT MANY LONG
HOURS CONTEMPLATING
THE CAMEMBERT

THERE WAS NO DENYING IT WAS INTERESTING, BUT WOULD IT BE ENOUGH TO SUSTAIN A LONG-TERM RELATIONSHIP?

AS HE REACHED THE FINAL
PARAGRAPH OF HIS MARRIAGE
PROPOSAL, BILLY NOTICED THAT
RUTH WAS NO LONGER THERE

AFTER A HEARTY BREAKFAST
TEX RETURNED TO HIS CHORES
IN THE GARDEN

LEON'S FORTH BRIDGE WAS BUT ONE
OF THE MANY HIGHLIGHTS OF
THAT WEEKEND IN TULSA

The Bungling at Dredgemere

CHANGING THE WHEEL FOR A RIVAL
WAS BUT ONE OF THE SELFLESS ACTS
WE AT ST. DRUNDLE'S PERFORMED...

BOYS WHO HAD FORGOTTEN THEIR
PROTRACTORS WERE SUBJECTED TO
MR LLOYD'S WALNUT ORDEAL

IN RECOGNITION OF MY OUTSTANDING
ACHIEVEMENTS ON THE FIELD, COACH
ALLOWED ME USE OF HIS TOWEL

WE WERE ALL IN AGREEMENT. AS AN
ACCOMPANIMENT TO CORNFLAKES IT
CERTAINLY MADE A REFRESHING CHANGE

ERIC WAS NOW BEGINNING TO WISH HE'D
RETURNED HIS OVERDUE LIBRARY BOOKS

"ONE REALLY MUST PAY ATTENTION
TO THE SHADING AT THE TIP OF
THE HORN, CECIL" ADVISED TIM

I LIKED TO THINK THAT MY
RELATIONSHIP WITH IRMA
WAS RATHER SPECIAL

I BEGAN TO SUSPECT THAT
MIRIAM WAS DELIBERATELY
SETTING OUT TO ANNOY ME

WHEN UNCLE NORMAN BEGAN TO
REMINISCE ABOUT THE
SIXTIES, TIM AND I WERE
FORCED TO PUT PLAN 'B'
INTO OPERATION

WITH DEADLY ACCURACY, ROBIN'S
FLASHLIGHT PICKED OUT THE
HIDDEN GOURDS

I WAS NOT TO FORGET MY FIRST
DETENTION WITH MR. BLISWORTH

SIXTEEN HOURS IN THE CELLAR BROUGHT
US TO OUR SENSES. WE AGREED TO STAY
AWAKE DURING THE REMAINING SLIDES
OF MR. BLUM'S DUTCH HIKING HOLIDAY

WE HAD PERFECTED OUR OWN
LITTLE WAY OF DEALING WITH
THOSE WHO SNEERED AT CORDUROY

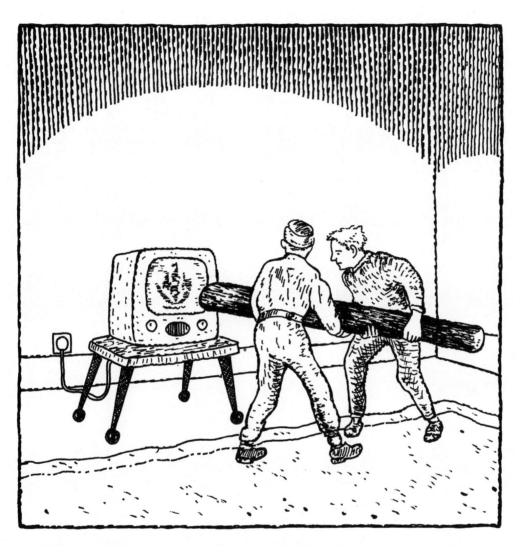

OUR FIRST MAJOR SUCCESS WAS AN
IN-DEPTH CRITICAL ANALYSIS OF
"BLUE PETER"...

OCCASIONALLY THE TERRIFYING WHIRR OF
THE PORRIDGE-MAKING FACILITIES COULD
BE HEARD DOWN THE CORRIDOR

THE BEST PART OF THE DAY WAS THE
SINGALONG ROUND THE SMOULDERING
REMAINS OF THE SCOUTMASTER'S
LUGGAGE...

"I'M AFRAID IT LOOKS LIKE
ANOTHER MASSIVE, OVERCOOKED
OMELETTE!" BARKED SNODE

I CERTAINLY IMPRESSED THE
LOCALS WHEN I BAGGED MY
FIRST MALE MOSQUITO.

TAKING A SNIFTER WITH BRIGADIER
TRENTWORTH PROVED TO BE A
DAUNTING EXPERIENCE

I THOUGHT IT PRUDENT TO ACCEPT
THE ADVICE OF THE LOCALS AND
OPT FOR THE CUTLETS.

"SO, CLUMPY McPHERSON! WE MEET
AGAIN, EH?" RASPED THE BURSAR.

"THIS DEFINITELY CONFIRMS THE EXISTENCE OF AN EARLIER, MORE PRIMITIVE SOCIETY!" BLURTED PENNINGTON

AS ASHTRAYS GO, IT WAS
CERTAINLY QUITE IMPRESSIVE

APPARENTLY OUR BILL FOR
TWO COFFEES DID CONTAIN
AN ELEMENT OF V.A.T

THE REDECORATION OF BASE CAMP
III WAS THE MOST PERILOUS ASPECT
OF THE ENTIRE EXPEDITION.

IT WAS TO BE QUITE A CHALLENGE.
WE HAD NEVER ATTEMPTED A
TWO-MAN ASCENT OF A FRAMED
WATERCOLOR SKETCH BEFORE.

WE ADVISED HIM AS TO WHERE
HE MIGHT PLACE HIS HERRING

"MY CAREER PROSPECTS MAY SEEM DIM,
CYNTHIA, BUT I WILL ALWAYS HAVE
MY TALENT!" BLURTED RODNEY

THERE WERE TIMES WHEN I BEGAN
TO TIRE OF POLISHING MR. THRONGUE

EACH WEEKEND I WAS SENT OFF
TO STAY WITH GRANDPARENTS

"SO DID YOU MANAGE TO RESOLVE
YOUR LITTLE DISAGREEMENT
WITH ERIC?" TRILLED THELMA

"I KNOW PRECISELY HOW TO START
AN ART APPRECIATION SOCIETY!"
SNORTED TIM TRIUMPHANTLY

I WAS DEALING WITH A DANGEROUS
MAN WHO AT ANY MOMENT MIGHT
BURST INTO A SELECTION FROM
"THE PAUL McCARTNEY SONGBOOK."

LIFE WITH HANS WAS NOT
ALWAYS A BOWL OF CHERRIES.